Becoming the People of God

Caring

for **God's**

Earth

By J. Richard Peck

Cokesbury / Nashville

02 03 04 05 06 07 08 09 10 11—10 9 8 7 6 5 4 3 2 1

Caring for God's Earth

Table of Contents

Introduction

Methodists have a long history of concern for the environment. John Wesley, the founder of the movement, expressed concern about open sewers, impure water, unplanned cities, and smoke-filled air. Wesley saw a relationship between sanitation and the presence of disease. The substantial decline in the death rate in England from 1700 to 1801 can be traced to improvements in environment, sanitation, and a wider knowledge of concepts of basic health. Wesley certainly contributed to those actions.

One hundred years later, the Methodist Church in America followed Wesley's example as members turned their attention to the environment. The first Social Creed, adopted by the 1908 General Conference of The Methodist Episcopal Church North, focused on health hazards facing workers. As the problems of soil erosion and dwindling reserves of natural resources became more obvious, subsequent General Conferences called for the development of programs stressing careful stewardship of the soil and conservation of natural resources.

At the 1968 union of the Methodist Church with the Evangelical United Brethren Church, the newly formed United Methodist Church expressed concern about pollution of the environment. The 1968 General Conference insisted that community rights take precedence over property rights and that "no individual should be permitted to degrade the environment . . . for the sake . . . of profit" (*The Book of Resolutions of The United Methodist Church, 1996;* pages 75–76). Every General Conference since the 1968 formation of The United Methodist Church has added or amended statements to the Social Principles and passes resolutions related to those principles.

Most of the Social Principles and resolutions are the result of individuals, local churches, or agencies writing petitions to be considered by the nearly 1,000 delegates to General Conference. These petitions are considered in legislative committees that recommend acceptance, rejection, or amendments. All delegates then vote on these recommendations.

The Preface to the Social Principles says they are "intended to be instructive and persuasive in the best of the prophetic spirit. [They are] a call to 9.4 million members of The United Methodist Church to a prayerful, studied dialogue of faith and practice." There is no need for readers to agree with every statement, and this book will offer suggestions for classes to address differences in opinion.

This book is organized into the seven units of The Natural World section (¶160) of the Social Principles with chapters under each unit. Some chapters also include resolutions related to the topic. All chapters contain suggestions for individual actions, reports on actions taken by local churches, and teaching plans for small groups.

It is unlikely that a study group will be able to use all the suggested activities in a single session, and leaders will probably want to continue the study of a chapter over several weeks. However, we hope that this book will not end with the study but will lead to appeals for legislation to protect the environment and individual actions to protect and nourish God's garden.

After you complete this study, you may want to seek others in the six-volume *Becoming the People of God* series. Check them out at *cokesbury.com* at your local Cokesbury store, or by calling Curric-U-Phone (800-251-8591).

Section One

Preface to The Natural World

SOCIAL PRINCIPLE ¶160

All creation is the Lord's, and we are responsible for the ways in which we use and abuse it. Water, air, soil, minerals, energy resources, plants, animal life, and space are to be valued and conserved because they are God's creation and not solely because they are useful to human beings. God has granted us stewardship of creation. We should meet these stewardship duties through acts of loving care and respect. Economic, political, social, and technological developments have increased our human numbers, and lengthened and enriched our lives. However, these developments have led to regional defoliation, dramatic extinction of species, massive human suffering, overpopulation, misuse and overconsumption of natural and nonrenewable resources, particularly by industrialized societies. This continued course of action jeopardizes the natural heritage that God has entrusted to all generations. Therefore, let us recognize the responsibility of the church and its members to place a high priority on changes in economic, political, social, and technological lifestyles to support a more ecologically equitable and sustainable world leading to a higher quality of life for all of God's creation.

God said, "Let the earth put forth vegetation: plants yielding seed, and fruit trees of every kind on earth that bear fruit with the seed in it." And God saw that it was good.—*Genesis 1:11-12*

The earth is the LORD's and all that is in it, / the world, and those who live in it. / for he has founded it upon the seas, / and established it on the rivers. —*Psalms 24:1*

9

Chapter 1

A Troubled Garden

Core Bible Passages

Genesis 1:11-31; Psalm 8; Psalm 24:1-2; Leviticus 25:2-7; Joel 2:21-27; Mark 4:26-29

In the first Creation story (Genesis 1:1–2:4a), God calls his creation "good." God does so before the creation of humankind (Genesis 1:24). Therefore, the Social Principles note that we need to care for the environment, not because it is useful to humankind, but because it is God's creation.

"In the Bible, a steward is one given responsibility for what belongs to another. The Greek word we translate as steward is *oikonomos*, one who cares for the household or acts as its trustee. The work *oikos*, meaning household, is used to describe the world as God's household. Christians, then, are to be stewards of the whole household (creation) of God" (*The Book of Resolutions, 2000*; page 88). To have dominion over the earth (Genesis 1:28) is to have a trusteeship that is accountable to God.

In the second Creation story (Genesis 2:4b-24) we find that when we violate the rules, we are condemned to leave the garden. Likewise, when we violate ecological rules, our existence is threatened. However, just as there is a consequence for sinful action, so there is a possibility for redemption. Contaminated lakes can be restored, and new trees can be planted in areas of deforestation.

In the Hebrew Scripture, "social, economic, and ecological justice with regard to the use of land was central to the law. The land itself was to receive a rest every seven years (Leviticus 25:4). Voluntary charity or occasional care of the land was not enough. Israel's failure to follow the laws related to the land was considered a cause of the exile to Babylon (2 Chronicles 36:21). The care of the land, the rights of the poor, and those in need were at the center of the law. Adequate food was regarded as an inherent right of all, such that the poor could eat grapes in a neighbor's vineyard or pluck grain when passing by a field (Deuteronomy 23:24-25). Owners were urged not to be too efficient in their harvest (Leviticus 19:9-10) so that gleaning by those in need was possible.

"Indeed, the concept of equal access to community resources according to need formed the basis of the covenant the community was expected to embody. The caring for one's neighbor especially one in need, became a religious obligation. Jesus both inherited and fulfilled this tradition when he listed the commandment to love your neighbor as yourself as second only to the commandment to love God (Matthew 22:38-40).

"The prophets saw the patterns of economic exploitation, social class consciousness, judicial corruption, political oppression, failing to care for the land, and exclusiveness as opposed to God's desire for full life and wholeness for all (Amos 2–8; Isaiah 5:1-13; 58:3-7; Jeremiah 2:7-8; Hosea 4:1-3). Some would suggest that both the contemporary world and Israel under the monarchy came to worship 'bigness' instead of God.

"Today, rural areas in our world suffer from many of the same maladies as did ancient Israel. Land holdings have become more concentrated. The accumulation of material wealth often is worshiped as the solution to other spiritual and economic problems. Creation itself groans under a burden of eroding topsoil, toxic wastes, and polluted waters."

(*Book of Resolutions, 2000*; pages 97–98)

Population Growth

The Social Principles note that economic, political, social, and technological developments have increased our human numbers, lengthened and enriched our lives.

Until about ten thousand years ago, the earth's capacity to support humans limited the number of people to a few million. Partially because of human efforts to grow crops and keep livestock, this number increased to nearly a half-billion in 1492. It took over 300 years for the population to double, reaching 1 billion in 1830. It then took one hundred years to again double, reaching 2 billion in 1930. By 2000, the world's population had reached 6 billion and scientists expect the earth to be host to 12 billion people by 2042. (*The Environment*, Abingdon Press, 1994; pages 17–18)

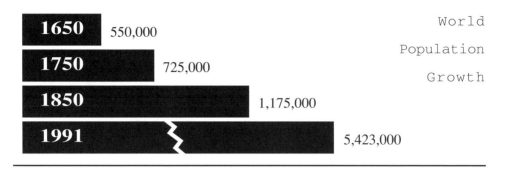

1650	550,000
1750	725,000
1850	1,175,000
1991	5,423,000

World Population Growth

Sanitation More Important Than Medical Care?

While medical science is given most of the credit for improved human longevity, data from United States Department of Health suggests we may owe more to the sanitation worker than to the family physician. (*The Golden Triangle,* by Robert L. Peck).

Table 1								
Death rates per 100,000 (National Center for Health Statistics, United States Dept. of Health and Human Services)								
	1900	1925	1950	1970	1980	1985	1990	1996
TB	185	97	23	3	1			
Heart	153	170	358	362	336	323	289	277
Cancers	68	87	140	163	184	193	202	05
Pneumonia	162	105	27	31	24	28	31	31
Diabetes	12	17	16	19	15	16	20	23
Measles	10	7	3					
All Causes	1621	1157	960	950	880	870	860	875

Other statistics indicate that death from smallpox, cholera, diphtheria, whooping cough, and measles were dropping steadily before vaccinations and antibiotics were introduced. After their development, the diseases continued to drop at the same rate as before and did not suddenly disappear as might have been predicted. It appears that increased sanitation practices may be more responsible for declining death rates for specific diseases than is medical science.

What Can a Local Church Do?

Recruit five- or six-member family groups to participate in the Household EcoTeam Program. The Global Action Plan, based in Woodstock, New York, sponsors the program.

This program simplifies the overload of environmental information and divides it into six specific areas—one set of actions to work on each month over a period of six months. An easy-to-use *Household EcoTeam Workbook* provides step-by-step guidance as an EcoTeam works through the monthly action areas.

The teams make selections from a series of practical action suggestions.

Action areas include

- Reduce your garbage;

- Improve home water efficiency;

- Improve home energy efficiency;

- Improve transportation efficiency;

- Be an eco-wise consumer;

- Empower others through household, workplace, and community actions;

- Sponsor a weekend experience at a local camp. The Web site: *www.gbod.org/camping* directory, lists church camps organized by annual conferences.

For information contact Global Action Plan, P.O. Box 428, Woodstock, NY 12498; E-mail: *http://www.globalactionplan.org;* Telephone 845-679-4830.

Teaching Plan

✓ *1. Begin with a prayer:* "God of the universe, when we consider the size and the magnitude of the universe, we ask, Why would you bother with us? We know you have given us life and, through your Son, you have shown us how to live on this planet. Help us to be sensitive to the presence of your Holy Spirit as we wrestle with ways we should respond to your gifts. In the name of Christ we pray."

2. Ask the class to study the two Creation stories. What are the differences? When was humankind created in Genesis 1:1-31? When was man created in Genesis 2:4-15? What difference does this make in our understanding about our place on earth?

3. Reflections. Ask the group: Does humankind have the ability to destroy the earth, or does God alone determine when the end is to come?

The General Conference of The United Methodist Church says that "Creation itself groans under a burden of eroding topsoil, toxic wastes, and polluted waters." What evidence of this suffering can we name?

4. Read the judgment of Hosea upon Israel (Hosea 4:1-6). What similarities exist in the world today?

5. Examine the graph of population growth on page 13. Can this planet support 12 billion people by 2042? Can our quality of life be maintained? What actions should be taken to reduce population?

6. Examine the chart on page 13. Why have deaths from heart disease and various forms of cancer increased while deaths from other diseases decreased? What impact do clean water, safe food, and proper waste disposal have on public health? What factors lead to an increase of heart disease and cancer?

Local Action Report

Church Street United Methodist Church in Knoxville, Tennessee, offers its 2,400 members an annual family retreat at a church-owned lodge in the mountains. Sue Isbell, who organizes the annual retreat, says the three-day experience allows participants to learn about the natural world and discover forgotten ways of living in harmony with God's creation.

Kevin Witt, national director for the United Methodist Camp/Retreat Ministry, believes that camp ministry experiences "serve as pathways to a deeper connection with God." He says that church camps enable participants "to relate lovingly with the earth and encourages people to return home to their churches with the knowledge and passion to support the earth as a sacred common ground for all."

Chapter 2

What Happened to the Family Farm?

(Paul E. Stroble contributed to this chapter.)

Core Bible Passages

Genesis 2:4b-9, 15; 3:17-19; 4:14; 47:13-26; Leviticus 25:2-7; Joel 2:21-27; Mark 4:26-32

The number of small farms that raised several kinds of crops and animals has declined sharply since 1950 due in part to the creation of larger, more specialized farms. Today, there are fewer than two million farms in the United States, down from 6.8 million in 1935. Formerly agricultural areas have been adopted for suburbs, industry, and other nonagricultural purposes, and smaller farms are being bought up as part of larger agribusinesses. Such social and economic changes push us to consider the overall food production for which we daily ask God's blessing.

The rural United States today is a contrast between beauty and desecration, isolation and industrialization, wealth and poverty, power and oppression, freedom and exploitation, abundance and hunger, and individualism and dependence. The nation's poorest housing and health facilities occur disproportionately in rural communities, as do the most inadequate education, the worst roads and transportation systems, the least progressive justice systems, and the greatest poverty and malnutrition.

Towns that not long ago were vibrant communities of economic, social, and spiritual life now have become ghost towns with empty businesses, abandoned homes, closed churches, and broken spirits. Broken homes, broken lives, suicides, bankruptcies, spouse and child abuse, unemployment, substance abuse and related violence, and other social catastrophes often make up the local news for many rural communities.

It is easy to be oblivious to the absence of family farms. Driving along the highway the farms appear serene, but behind the facade are hundreds of thousands of tons of manure from hog and chicken operations. These waste products are stored in lagoons that foul the air and pollute the water. These same livestock operations often receive subsidies from the federal and state governments causing a shift in the tax burden to other agricultural property owners, thus driving family farms out of business.

World Trade and the Family Farm

There are many who believe global trade in United States farm products is the best way to help farmers and feed the hungry around the world.

Judith Heffernan, executive director of the Heartland Network for Town and Rural Ministries, disagrees:

"In economic theory this belief might hold true," she says, "but for farmers producing for the global market, the reality differs. While the politically and economically powerful transnational grain, meat, and food corporations that control global trade enjoy high returns on their investments, commodity prices flounder below the cost of production. Farmers everywhere are either forced off their land or become dependent on supplemental payments from government to stay in business.

"The question those of us in the United States should be asking," she says, "is whether or not we will soon stop feeding ourselves and what it will mean if we do" (*Response*, February 2001; page 26).

Heffernan also notes that some economists believe that United States farmers are no longer needed. They suggest we buy food from poor nations and use our land for other purposes. "Eating food produced by the poor in developing countries who have insufficient food for their own families raises major moral and ethical questions," says Heffernan. "Christians are realizing that we can no longer allow the needs and values of the marketplace enacted into public policy to trump all other needs of God's creation."

Farm Facts

■ According to the United States Department of Agriculture, there are now 1.91 million farms in the United States, about the same number as in the 1992 report. Prior to that, the last year this nation had fewer than 2 million farms was in 1850. In 1935, the nation had 6.8 million farms. With the advent of corporate farms, 2 percent of the farms now produce 50 percent of agricultural product sales.

- Between 1993 and 1997, the number of mid-sized family farms decreased by 74,440.

- These figures indicate a loss of the smaller operations that once typified American agriculture. However, 86 percent of American farms are still owned and operated by individuals or families. Seventy percent of farm workers are family members; the other 30 percent are hired workers.

- Nearly half of all farmers are over age 55, while just 8 percent are under age 35.

- The farmer's share of each food dollar has dropped steadily over the last 40 years, from 41 cents in 1950 to only 20 cents in 1999. Meanwhile, farm machinery is very expensive. A new combine, for example, may cost a quarter million dollars. In 1998, farmers earned an average of only $7,000 per year from their farming operations.

- Of American food prices as reflected at the grocery store, about 20 percent is for the food itself. Eighty percent is for processing and marketing.

- Declining land values, the relationship between farm product prices and incomes, farm debt and bankruptcies, forced land transfers and foreclosures, changes in the structure of agriculture, and tax policy continue to contribute to the loss of family farms.

Basic Directions That Must Be Changed

- The movement toward investor-owned land in increasingly larger corporate units; the separation of ownership, management, and labor;

- The increased reliance upon high inputs of nonrenewable resources such as fossil fuels and chemicals;

- The continued decline in rural populations from rural areas, especially those who have been directly involved in food production;

- The increasing chemical toxicity of our water systems, air, rain, waste dumps, and vegetable and animal products;

- The continuing loss of cropland through erosion, salinization, urbanization, conversion, and other processes;

- The disappearance of world forest resources and the resulting changes in weather patterns;

- The loss of our centuries-old genetic seed bank.

(From *The Book of Resolutions, 2000*; page 107)

Three Ethical Guidelines

We can change the direction of agriculture and rural development, but we need guidelines. A preferred agriculture must have three attributes:

- It must be *just*. A just society and a just agriculture provide the means whereby people can share in the inheritance of the earth so that all life can fully be maintained in freedom and community. The purpose of a just agriculture should be for the maintenance and renewal of the necessary resources for food, clothing, and shelter, for now and for the future.

- It must be *participatory*. For agriculture to be just, everyone has the right to be consulted. Participation in society and in the ongoing process of creation is the necessary condition for justice. Participation requires recognition of everyone's right to be consulted and understood, regardless of that person's economic, political, or social status. Participation is not possible without power. In such decision-making, everyone has the right to be consulted about such issues as expenditures for armaments, nuclear power, forms of employment, social services, and so forth.

- It must be *sustainable*. A sustainable agriculture is one where the idea of permanent carrying capacity is maintained, where yields (agriculture, energy production, forestry, water use, industrial activity) are measured by whether or not they are sustainable rather than by the criteria of yields per acre or profits. In a sustainable agriculture, waste products can be absorbed back into the ecosystem without damage.

(From *The Book of Resolutions, 2000*; page 107–08)

Farm Policy After the Attack on America

Following the September 11, 2001, attack upon the World Trade Center and the Pentagon, Bill Christison, president of the National Family Farm Coalition, said the events "have placed a new urgency on the necessity of enacting a new federal agriculture policy, on the issues around food security and food sovereignty.

"We as family farmers, have always provided food security for our nation," said Christison. "We also believe the people of the United States deserve food sovereignty because food sovereignty fosters the economic, political, and cultural sovereignty of the people. Furthermore, food sovereignty entails the recognition and appreciation of the economic, social, environmental, and cultural advantages of small-scale family farmers."

Christison backs food sovereignty because he thinks present trade policy promotes one country dumping produce in another with prices below the cost of production. He argues that present policy has cost the United States workers 750,000 jobs. "Fair Trade policy cannot be achieved unless both the producers and consumers are represented at the table."

What Can a Local Church Do?

In some areas the churches have been helpful in assisting farmers to cope with the loss of their farms and in aiding others to help keep their farms. Unfortunately, in many cases, churches have been ineffective in fulfilling this ministry. A number of reasons have been cited for the church's shortcoming:

- Many church members accept a theology that "goodness" means "success," and that failure means that God has punished the person for his or her "sins."

- Many clergy are not adequately trained to minister to the needs of the hurting families in their communities.

- In general, clergy are more involved in responding to congregational needs than to the needs of the larger community.

- In many rural areas, churches are still operating under an independent rather than a cooperative model.

Local churches are asked to

- Take responsibility for assisting with mending the brokenness of community life in rural society;

- Strengthen their ministry and mission with rural churches and communities;

- Lift up the responsible stewardship of natural resources;

- Build bridges of understanding and partnership between rural and urban congregations and communities;

- Become public policy advocates, creating awareness and understanding, and bringing about positive change;

- Sponsor volunteers-in-mission teams in rural areas;
- Recognize Rural Life Sunday as a special day in the church year (*The Book of Resolutions, 2000*; pages 100–04);
- Support legislation backed by the National Family Farm Coalition (*http://www.nffc.net*).

Teaching Plan

1. Begin with a prayer: "Forgive us God for neither knowing nor caring about the source of our daily bread. Help us to be sensitive to the needs of farmers and their families. Guide us as we consider ways in which we can be of help to those struggling to maintain their way of life. In the name of Christ we pray."

2. Reflect. In 1935, there were 6.8 million farms compared to 2 million today. Ask: What does this statistic mean to our way of life, to family farms, and to the economy? What does this change mean for the church?

3. Consider. Only 20 percent of the amount we pay for food goes to the farmer; the rest of the cost is for processing, packaging, and marketing. Illustrate this fact by stacking ten slices of bread and removing two. Ask: How much labor does the farmer put into the product compared to those who receive 80 percent of the purchase price?

4. Consider statements by the 2000 General Conference related to basic directions that need changing (page 19) and ethical guidelines (page 20). Ask: Do you agree with these proposals? What directions or ethical guidelines would you add or delete?

5. Reread the story of Cain and Abel. Why was the offering of Cain (a tiller of the land) not acceptable?

6. Read Genesis 47:13-26. How does the story of Joseph in the years of famine relate to small family farms today?

Local Action Reports

Ed Kail, pastor of Faith United Methodist Church in Humboldt, Iowa, says the restructuring of agriculture in that area is nearly complete. " 'Saving the family farm' is an out-of-date slogan in this area," says Kail. Most of the people with family farms earn their living in some other occupation and engage in farming on a part-time basis, or they have sold out to one of the local industries. He reports that five years ago about 30 percent of the farmers in Wayne County, Iowa, were working part-time on their farms; today about 70 percent are part-time farmers.

Kail says he now tries to provide basic spiritual support to those who are no longer full-time farmers. He also works through ecumenical groups, such as the National Farm Coalition, to have an impact on federal legislation. "The transition to industrial agribusiness is now complete," says Kail. "Everything is now judged by profit and the bottom line with no regard for Christian or even humanistic values. As president of The United Methodist Rural Fellowship, Kail is also urging United Methodists to address concerns about the environment. He notes that large industrial farms are sterilizing the soil and contaminating the water. "The issue of water quality is a ticking time bomb," he said.

Carol Thompson, executive director of the Western Small-Church Rural Life Center in Lyons, Oregon, has spent most of the year helping churches address issues involved in a boycott of a packing facility by Hispanic farm workers. The Oregon-Idaho Annual Conference of The United Methodist Church supported the boycott from June 2000 to June 2001. Thompson said she is also encouraging churches to get to know Hispanic farm workers in their areas and possibly host English-as-a-Second-Language (ESL) classes. She is also urging churches to look at the health system, early childhood education, housing, and school systems with regard to Hispanic farm workers.

Silverton (Oregon) United Methodist Church hosts an English-as-a-Second-Language class for migrant farm workers. Church members provide childcare while parents attend classes. Steve Mitchell, pastor of the 196-member congregation, says the church works with Silverton Together, a group of religious and civic organizations, to provide food for migrant and low-income families in the community. The church also provides a cooking class for

Latinos, who learn to cook and speak English at the same time. When it rains or the weather is stormy, the church provides an indoor park where parents and their toddlers can play with toys, tricycles, balls, climbing bars, and mats.

First United Methodist Church in Walters, Oklahoma, calls itself "the friendliest church in town." Members welcome visitors and always follow up with home visits, inviting visitors to become part of "our faith family." First Church leads the community-wide food drive and serves as the location for the year-round food closet, which provided more than 50 families with holiday food baskets last year. Members drive for "Meals on Wheels" and help with "Eldercare." A cooperative preschool operates in the church. The church serves as a community center by hosting blood drives, AA meetings, school events, family reunions, and service club meetings. The church was awarded a "Heartland Network" award for rural ministry.

Water, Air, Soil, Minerals, Plants

SOCIAL PRINCIPLE ¶160A

We support and encourage social policies that serve to reduce and control the creation of industrial byproducts and waste; facilitate the safe processing and disposal of toxic and nuclear waste and move toward the elimination of both; encourage reduction of municipal waste; provide for appropriate recycling and disposal of municipal waste; and assist the cleanup of polluted air, water, and soil. . . . We support measures designed to maintain and restore natural ecosystems. We support policies that develop alternatives to chemicals used for growing, processing, and preserving food, and we strongly urge adequate research into their effects upon God's creation prior to utilization. We urge development of international agreements concerning equitable utilization of the world's resources for human benefit so long as the integrity of the earth is maintained.

Then God said, "Let us make humankind in our image, according to our likeness; and let them have dominion over the fish of the sea, and over the birds of the air, and over the cattle, and over all the wild animals of the earth, and over every creeping thing that creeps upon the earth."—*Genesis 1:26*

 I have set before you life and death, blessing and curses. Choose life so that you and your descendants may live, loving the LORD your God, obeying him, and holding fast to him; for that means life to you and length of days.—*Deuteronomy 30:19b-20a*

Chapter 3

Is the End at Hand?

(Paul E. Stroble and Pamela Dilmore contributed to this chapter.)

Core Bible Passages

Genesis 1:26; Jeremiah 4:23-26; Revelation 8:6–9:21; Revelation 21–22

There are several hypotheses related to the extinction of the dinosaurs. Several years ago, Luis and Walter Alvarez, father and son, discovered a high concentration of the element iridium in a sediment sample from a rock layer representing the time the dinosaurs became extinct, 65 million years ago. Soil samples from around the world showed similar amounts of iridium, which is common in meteorites but rare on earth. The Alvarezes estimate that a meteorite about six miles across could account for this worldwide distribution of iridium.

Then, in the early 1990s, a crater was discovered near the Mexican village of Chicxulub. The crater—long undiscovered because it is covered with sediment—is about 110 miles wide (the estimated size that would have been left by a six-mile-wide meteorite) and 65 million years old. The Alvarezes theorize that the asteroid threw dust into the atmosphere, which blotted out the sun, killing plants, then dinosaurs and other species of animals.

Other scientists theorize that the presence of iridium can be explained by volcanic activity. They suspect such activity occurred around the "Deccan Traps" in India, causing an increase in carbon dioxide, which in turn created global warming.

The dinosaurs were not the only mass extinction. Eighty percent of life died 248 million years ago, making way for the dinosaurs. An earlier cycle of extinction was 650 million years ago, when algae and aquatic bacteria died off. A mass extinction of mammal life occurred about 11 million years ago.

Without Comets or Volcanoes

Environmentalists today are less fearful of comets or volcanoes than they are of the consequences of our own habits. Many believe that the burning of fossil fuels is building up man-made carbon dioxide in the atmosphere and creating another cycle. Recent increases in average temperatures seem to be related to increasing amounts of carbon dioxide in the atmosphere, caused by burning fossil fuels. A blanket of carbon dioxide, water vapor, methane, and other gasses covers the earth and entraps heat. As carbon dioxide levels increase, the blanket thickens, and more heat is trapped. If warming increases, the results could be catastrophic for forests, coastal areas (where the sea level could rise), and food production. Other scientists write about similar effects caused by acid rain.

Ecosystems do not show immediate damage but absorb it over a period of time. Our own bodies react the same way. Forests do not die immediately when exposed to acid rain, but eventually severe damage results. The cumulative damage eventually reaches a critical point and the collapse of the ecosystem can be catastrophic. Environmentalists ask whether global warming, ozone, ultraviolet radiation, pesticides, and other toxins will someday create disastrous consequences upon food production and, thus, upon human and animal life.

The View From Revelation

The Book of Revelation depicts the end of time. Revelation 8:6–9:21 describes the angels who blow the seven trumpets to initiate various cosmic disasters. The earth suffers under the destruction of hail and fire that strikes the earth, the trees and grass, the seas and rivers, and the heavenly bodies. The sea becomes blood, and living plants and creatures are consumed by fire. Following the fiery blast comes a plague of monstrous locusts, torturing and then killing the unfaithful; but not all is lost.

In Revelation 21–22, the first earth passes away; and God brings about a new heaven and a new earth, wherein sorrow, suffering, and evil belong to the past. God's glory substitutes for the sun's light. The tree of life amid the river of the water of life produces fruit "for the healing of the nations." The whole book is a long disaster epic, and God's lordship provides us with both a warning and comfort.

Ecology Facts

- In 1997, the average American contributed 1,570 pounds of solid trash and 3,613 pounds of sewage to the environment. This growth of accumulated waste exceeds nature's ability to break it down.

■ It takes a glass bottle approximately 1 million years to decompose; an aluminum can, 200–500 years; a painted wood stake, 13 years; a cotton rag, 1 to 5 months, and an orange peel, 2 to 5 weeks.

■ Cigarette filters are composed of cellulose acetate, a form of plastic. Estimates on how long it takes them to decompose range from a few months to 5 years to never. They may decompose faster than disposable diapers, which need 450 years to decompose, but millions of people don't throw diapers out of their car windows.

■ Acid rain, which can leach away the color in car paint and corrode marble into dust, is caused by sulfur dioxide in the air. While the chemical occurs naturally, the burning of fossil fuels is the major culprit for about half of the emissions of this gas around the world. Sulfur dioxide and nitrogen dioxide emissions can cause respiratory problems. Acid rain leaches toxic metals into water, which are absorbed by plants and then consumed by humans who eat those plants. Indirectly, acid rain has been linked with brain damage, nerve disorders, and death.

■ Even treated water has toxins in it, including solid waste. Each state receives a water quality report from the Environmental Protection Agency. In the state of Washington, 60 percent of the rivers, 65 percent of lakes, and 44 percent of estuarine waters do not support aquatic life uses. Among the most significant pollutants in ground water are nitrates, pesticides, agricultural chemicals, and human waste from septic tanks.

■ According to a study by the Pesticide Action Network North America, the use of cancer-causing pesticides in California has more than doubled in eight years, up 127 percent from 1991 to 1998. People most at risk from this pesticide use are farm workers who come into direct contact with the chemicals in the fields.

A Dioxin-Free Future

The United States Environmental Protection Agency's (EPA) 1994 report entitled "The Scientific Reassessment of Dioxin" affirmed health warnings made twenty years ago—that the "background" levels of dioxin, a deadly chlorine-based chemical, pose a serious threat to the health of the general United States population.

The EPA concluded that dioxin compounds cause several types of cancer. Exposure to toxic chemicals such as dioxin is widely suspected to be related to the increasing rates of cancer in the United States. The rate of testicular cancer has tripled in the past thirty years, the rate of prostate cancer has doubled in the past ten years, and the rate of breast cancer in the United States has risen from one in every twenty women in the 1960s to one in every eight women today. More women have died of breast cancer in the last two decades than the number of United States soldiers killed in World War I, World War II, and the Korean and Vietnam wars combined.

The EPA report stated that there is reason to believe that dioxins at extremely low levels cause a wide range of other serious health effects, including reproductive impairment, learning disabilities, developmental injuries, and the increased risk of diabetes and endometriosis. Furthermore, even low levels of dioxin impair the ability of the immune system to fight infectious disease. The EPA report says that there is no level of dioxin below which the immune system is not affected.

The EPA concluded that the levels of dioxins already lodged in human bodies are already close to levels known to cause serious health problems. According to the EPA, the average person is exposed to dioxin levels 50 to 100 times greater than the maximum allowable amounts designated by the federal government in 1985.

Some persons have what the EPA calls "special" exposures, including certain occupational groups; people living near dioxin emitters; and people who consume higher than average levels of meat, fish, and dairy products. Human exposure to dioxins begins early in life, since dioxin crosses the placenta. Nursing infants take in four to twelve percent of their lifetime dose of dioxin within the first year of their lives, a period during which they are most susceptible to the effects of such toxins.

Toxic pollution costs society hundreds of billions of dollars each year in expenses for health care, diminished productivity, waste disposal, and remediation of contaminated sites and ground water.

A healthy population, a clean environment, and efficient, nonpolluting technologies are essential to a sound economy. "With a single program—dioxin phaseout—much of the world's most severe toxic pollution could be stopped" (*The Book of Resolutions, 2000;* pages 68–70).

What Can a Local Church Do?

- Urge cancer research organizations to move to a prevention-based approach to cancer research and funding, including more studies on the relationship between cancer and chlorine-based toxins in the environment.

- Support a phase-out of the production of dioxin, beginning with the immediate action on the three largest sources of dioxin: incineration of chlorine-containing wastes, bleaching of pulp and paper with chlorine, and the entire life-cycle of polyvinyl chloride (PVC) plastic.

- Urge health-care facilities to reduce or eliminate their use of PVC plastics.

- Support worker protection programs for people working in industries that make toxic chemicals or result in toxic by-product and related chemicals, who may lose their jobs with a phase-out of these chemicals. Such programs could include a "Workers' Superfund" program.

Teaching Plan

1. Discuss. Ask the group to discuss the meaning of the word *dominion* in Genesis 1:26. What are some factors involved in human beings having dominion over creation? What is the difference between *dominion* and *domination*?

2. Bible study. Form three groups and assign each group a passage of Scripture: Jeremiah 4:23-26 (What is the vision of the natural world? What is happening to it? Who is in control of it?); Revelation 8:6–9:21 (Who are the principal actors in this passage? What are they doing? What is the result?); and Revelation 21–22 (What does John see? How is it different from what has gone before?).

3. Reflect. Are natural events the instruments of God's punishment, the natural result of sin and evil, or the result of chance? Is there a relationship between humankind's treatment of the world and the scenario of Scripture? If God is in control of the end, does this mean that people do not have to be responsible for their actions?

4. Study Psalm 104. List some images of the natural world that can be found in the psalm. Is there any ecological advice in the psalms, or does the psalmist merely observe and appreciate God's creation?

5. Thank God for the joys and peace that you have gained from your favorite natural places in the world. Thank God for the air, clean water, food, and other blessings.

Local Action Reports

Susan Mackenzie, 41, remembers developing "a strong kinship with creation" as a child at an outdoor family church camp. Since then, the member of Pleasant Street Church, Waterville, Maine, has become instrumental in various environmental issues and programs in the state. Director of the Spirituality and Earth Stewardship Program of the Maine Council of Churches, she was honored with the 1999 Sierra Club Award for "Leadership in Promoting Conservation at the Grassroots Level." Yet, when asked her greatest accomplishment, the mother of two says it's teaching her children the importance of preserving nature.

The Lutheran Church of the Reformation in a Minneapolis suburb committed itself to making "Care for the Creation" central to its life and mission over the next five years.

"The church has set a new course toward becoming an 'eco-church,'" said Pastor Dennis Ormseth, a former seminary professor. "In partnership with our neighbors, we have developed a community garden on part of our property." Ormseth says the garden models "the kind of environmental stewardship that will sustain a living earth for generations to come." Ormseth emphasizes ecological issues in his preaching and teaching, and the congregation plans to transform nearby woods into a model wildlife habitat.

A dozen members of Broadway United Methodist Church decided they could play a role in turning around "one of the worst neighborhoods" in Indianapolis. They went door to door in an effort to determine the needs and skills of residents. They then coordinated efforts to renovate a community center, sponsor neighborhood cleanups, and sponsor a community vegetable and flower garden.

Price Hill United Methodist Church in Cincinnati joined with three neighboring churches in the deteriorating neighborhood to address ecological issues. They began with comprehensive energy audits of their own facilities. In cooperation with a neighborhood ecological-education organization, the churches helped plant thousands of trees throughout the community. The group also received a $20,000 grant from the city to purchase eight acres of land for an "Outdoor Earth Lab" for children in the ten schools located within a mile of the property. The land helps students to see how their lifestyles affect the earth and to see the earth as a sacred place. The group also sponsors a "Festival for the Earth."

Chapter 4

Is the Earth Warming?

Core Bible Passages

Genesis 7:1–9:17 (focus: 8:22)

According to the Environmental Protection Agency, global mean surface temperatures have increased 0.5 to 1.0°F since the late-nineteenth century. The ten warmest years have all occurred in the last fifteen years. Of these, 1998 was the warmest year on record. The snow cover in the northern hemisphere and floating ice in the Arctic Ocean have decreased. Globally, the sea level has risen 4 to 8 inches over the past century. Worldwide precipitation over land has increased by about one percent. The frequency of extreme rainfall events has increased throughout much of the United States. The increasing concentration of greenhouse gases is likely to accelerate the rate of climate change. Scientists expect that the average global surface temperature could rise 1 to 4.5°F (0.6 to 2.5°C) in the next fifty years and 2.2 to 10°F (1.4 to 5.8°C) in the next century, with significant regional variation. Evaporation will increase as the climate warms, which will increase average global precipitation. Soil moisture is likely to decline in many regions, and intense rainstorms are likely to become more frequent. Sea level could rise two feet along most of the United States coast.

Why are greenhouse gas concentrations increasing? Scientists generally believe that the combustion of fossil fuels and other human activities are the primary reason for the increased concentration of carbon dioxide. Plant respiration and the decomposition of organic matter release more than 10 times the carbon dioxide released by human activities; but these releases have generally been in balance during the centuries leading up to the industrial revolution with carbon dioxide absorbed by terrestrial vegetation and the oceans.

What has changed in the last few hundred years is the additional release of carbon dioxide by human activities. Fossil fuels burned to run cars and trucks, heat homes and businesses, and power factories are responsible for about 98 percent of United States carbon dioxide emissions, 24 percent of methane emissions, and 18 percent of nitrous oxide emissions. Increased agriculture, deforestation, landfills, industrial production, and mining also contribute a significant share of emissions. While the population of the United States

34

comprises only 4 percent of the global community, we contribute 20 percent of all greenhouse gas emissions.

Estimating future emissions is difficult, because it depends on demographic, economic, technological, policy, and institutional developments. Several emissions scenarios have been developed based on differing projec-tions of these underlying factors. For example, by 2100, in the absence of emissions control policies, carbon dioxide concentrations are projected to be 30 to 150 percent higher than today's levels. (United States Environmental Protection Agency Position Paper)

The Intergovernmental Panel on Climate Change, composed of 2,500 scientists from around the world, claims that whether or not global warming exists is no longer the issue. The report states with "most confidence" that the twentieth century was the warmest in the last 1,000 years, heating is consistent around the globe, and 90 percent of all local changes in temperature coincide with biological changes in plants and animals in surrounding areas.

While the population of the United States comprises only 4 percent of the global community, this nation contributes 20 percent of all greenhouse gas emissions. Due to its wealth, the United States is one of the countries best positioned to reduce the impact of global warming in the future and to protect other nations and itself from its present effects.

Not all developed countries have failed to control greenhouse gas emissions. Through fuel-efficient vehicles, conservation, and alternative energy, Germany has decreased carbon dioxide emissions by more than 20 percent in the last ten years. In the same period of time, the United States, by continuing to rely primarily on fossil fuels for its energy use, has increased emissions by 13 percent. (*Christian Social Action*, September–October, 2001—article by Amanda Glenn)

A Contrary Point of View

Not everyone is convinced that global warming is the result of human action. Writing in *Natural History* magazine (October 2001), Wallace S. Broecker finds there was a "little ice age," a cold period that ran from about 1300 to 1860.

The scientist agrees that a century and a half ago, the world's mountainous regions were somewhat colder than they are today. He documents this with historical records and early photographs that show the glaciers were larger then. However, he is not certain that humanity has contributed to this warming trend.

He notes that roughly half the overall warming since 1860 occurred before carbon dioxide (CO_2) emissions from human activities had reached significant levels.

In spite of his doubts about the role of human activity in global warming, Broecker says we dare not sit back and do nothing and wait for more information. "In twenty years, we may well conclude that we must stem the rise of CO_2, and if so, we've got a lot of preparation to do," he writes.

Broecker suggests that with more people and higher standards of living the demand for energy will double by the year 2050. "We must learn how to remove CO_2 from power-plant exhausts and probably from the atmosphere itself."

"We have learned that Holocene temperatures have undergone natural fluctuations," writes Broecker, "but the causes of these changes are so subtle that we have yet to figure them out. Apparently, our climate system responds to even tiny nudges. This being the case, the potential effects of human activities should not be underestimated. If we continue along a business-as-usual energy course, we'll be giving the climate a large shove."

What Can One Person Do?

The EPA suggests the following actions for individuals:

Inside the Home: Purchase energy-efficient appliances and home equipment. A front-loading washing machine uses a third less water and detergent than the typical top-loading model. Look for the "Energy Star" label. Replace incandescent light bulbs with compact fluorescent lights. Improve home insulation. Save on water use. Consider a solar thermal system to heat household water.

In the Yard: Plant deciduous trees. Use plants that require little watering. Use a composting lawnmower. Minimize waste sent to a landfill.

At the Store: Recycle. Buy products with reusable or recyclable packaging or recycled content.

On the Road: Plan and organize errands to one trip. Consider transportation alternatives such as public transportation, walking, or bicycling. Maintain automobiles in proper tune with tires inflated to correct pressures. Carpool and telecommute when possible. Purchase fuel efficient automobiles and vehicles.

Everywhere: Educate others about ways to save money and protect the environment

What Can a Local Church Do?

- Help educate the congregation about environmental issues.

- Create a meditation garden.

- Plant a tree on church grounds or in the community for each new child baptized.

- Dedicate the regular children's hour to studying God's creation.

- Move church services outdoors.

- Plan regular environmental "clean-up" days for youth and adults.

- Cooperate with church camps to offer programs that tie faith with environmental responsibility.

- Explore issues of consumption, justice, and faith with junior high and high school students

- Form an youth ecology group and study *Beyond Leaf Raking: Learning to Serve/Serving to Learn,* by Peter L. Benson and Eugene C. Roehlkepartain (Abingdon Press, 1993).

- Form an adult ecology group and study *Caring for God's World*, edited by Kristen Kemper (Educational Ministries, 1991).

- Include ecological concerns in your parish newsletter.

- Stop using disposable utensils at church dinners.

- Host a nature hike.

- See additional resources on the Web at 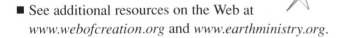 *www.webofcreation.org* and *www.earthministry.org.*

Teaching Plan

1. Open with a prayer: "God of the earth, the sun, and the stars, we confess that we are confused about our role in global warming and we seek your guidance. Give us clarity of vision and use us as your instruments. In Christ's name we pray."

2. Read the story of Noah (Genesis 7–9:17).

3. Discuss: In the light of global warming should residents of island nations and maritime communities imitate Noah and begin to protect themselves from impending floods? Does God's promise in Genesis guarantee there will be no flooding of individual nations?

4. Stage a debate between two persons portraying scientists. One person will claim that global warming is caused by human behavior, the other will argue it is the result of a natural cycle.

5. Ask: If scientists can't agree on whether global warming is caused by human behavior, should we wait for more information before we take action?

Local Action Report

The Rev. Frank Shields, minister of the Sunnyside United Methodist Church in East Portland, Oregon, is also a member of the Oregon state legislature who is concerned about global warming. "We're in deep denial in this country," he said.

Shields, who is vice chairman of the environment and energy committee of the Oregon legislature, said people "do not want to admit that we have an effect" on the climate. "There are individual things people can do," he stressed.

When people have a short drive to work, they release less carbon dioxide into the air—an important factor in global warming. If their car gets 32 miles to the gallon instead of 15, that is cutting the emission of this gas in half, he said. Using public transportation is even better, he added. Portland has done a lot with mass transit and is developing light rail trains, he said, but an essential factor is the effort "to contain our urban growth boundary."

"Some of the most fertile land in the world is located just outside that boundary," Shields said, "so the law reserves it for farming. When there is pressure to extend the urban boundary for development, the discussion takes place in a public forum and hilly sections not good for agriculture are rezoned for building. Fertile land is preserved in exclusive farm-use zones."

Instead of urban sprawl, the city has "very pleasant neighborhoods" that Shields likens to those of a European city.

"It's a wonderful city to live in," he declared.

Oregon, he said, has led the way in legislation, having been one of the first states to pass a bottle law—which requires beverages to be packaged in recyclable containers with a mandatory deposit to encourage their return—and the first to legislate against the use of chlorofluorocarbons, ozone-depleting gasses.

Business keeps urging slow or no change, predicting dire consequences for the economy, Shields said. But, he stated, this year Oregon passed a law requiring new power plants to be built with a 17 percent reduction in greenhouse emissions. The bipartisan environment and energy committee wrote the bill.

"Nobody's panicked about it," he said. "Utility prices haven't been affected."

Church leaders in North Carolina have issued a statement on global warming through the North Carolina Council of Churches. The statement, signed by 35 judicatory leaders, urges churches to (1) distribute educational materials; (2) offer presentations and convene study groups to help our communities understand the negative impact on the earth of some personal behaviors and lifestyles; and (3) take action to conserve energy and reduce waste and use of fossil fuels. The group also declares support for the United States Senate ratification of the Kyoto Protocol, "thereby joining in an international effort to address the threat of climate change."

Chapter 5

Racism and the Environment

Core Bible Passages

Psalms 77; 79; 109; Proverbs 14:20

A generally ignored aspect of any study on the natural world is environmental racism. The General Conference of The United Methodist Church notes that people of color are disproportionately affected by toxic contamination due to the production, storage, treatment, and disposal process of hazardous materials and wastes (*The Book of Resolutions, 2000;* pages 84–87). African American, Hispanic North American, Asian American, Native American, and Third World communities are usually the least able, politically and economically, to oppose the location of these facilities.

Research has documented the following:

1. According to a study by the United Church of Christ, race is consistently the most statistically significant variable in the location of commercial hazardous waste facilities. Three of the five largest commercial hazardous waste landfills in the United States are located in communities of color. Communities with commercial hazardous waste facilities have two to three times the average minority population of communities without such facilities. Three out of every five African Americans and Hispanic North Americans live in communities with toxic waste sites. The predominantly African American and Hispanic south side of Chicago has the greatest concentration of hazardous waste sites in the United States.

2. Communities where hazardous waste incinerators are located tend to have large minority populations, low incomes, and low property values. The minority portion of the population in communities with existing incineration is 98 percent higher than the national average. In Houston, Texas, six of eight municipal incinerators and 15 of the 16

landfills are located in predominantly African American neighborhoods.

3. Communities of color have greater cancer rates than white communities. Many environmental groups are calling for a study of possible causal relationship between environmental contamination and increased cancer rates.

4. Fifty percent of the children in the United States suffering from lead poisoning are African American.

5. Farm workers' children (mainly Hispanics) in the United States suffer a higher rate of birth defects due to their mothers' exposure to pesticides during the early stages of pregnancy. In farm worker communities, children with cancer are common. Pesticide exposure among farm workers causes more than 300,000 pesticide-related illnesses each year.

6. Navajo teenagers have cancer rates seventeen times the national average due to countless uranium spills on Navajo lands that have contaminated the water, air, and soil.

7. The growing trend during the 1980s and 1990s has been to dump toxic wastes in developing countries. Countries such as Liberia have been offered much-needed foreign capital to accept shipments of toxic wastes in the past few years. Unfortunately, these countries often lack the appropriate infrastructure to handle the environmental and health problems adequately that accompany these wastes.

Our society's attitude toward the production and disposal of hazardous products is one of "out of sight, out of mind." But "out of sight, out of mind" is most often where the poor and powerless live and work. These communities have thus become toxic "sacrifice zones." This pattern of racism represents a serious challenge to the conscience of all Christians.

Black-Owned Farmland

"Today you have driven me away from the soil."—*Genesis 4:14*

In 1920, the United States had over 925,000 black-operated farms. Today there are fewer than 18,500. The current rate of agricultural loss by black farmers is over two times that of other American farmers.

Compared to other groups, black farmers depend more heavily on farming for an income and have less off-farm income. The continuing loss of ownership and control of agricultural land by black American farmers has reduced their ability to achieve economic viability and financial independence. This loss has been accelerated by the black landowners' lack of access to capital, technical information, and legal resources needed to retain and develop agricultural land holdings into stable, income-producing, self-sustaining operations.

The 2000 General Conference accused the United States Department of Agriculture (USDA) of practicing "widespread discrimination [that] cost black farmers loan approval, loan servicing, and farm management assistance."

In 1999, the USDA agreed to a $50,000-per-person settlement of a class-action suit by African American farmers. The department also agreed to forgive the debts of qualified black farmers who were denied government loans and other assistance because of their race. Unfortunately that settlement came too late for many black farmers who had already lost their lands.

General Conference urged the USDA "to put into place stringent regulations to guard against discrimination, and to include black and other minority farmers on county committees that oversee USDA loans and other programs" (*The Book of Resolutions, 2000*; pages 548–50).

Hate Groups in Rural Communities

Hate groups thrive in rural settings. They accuse people of color of displacing whites in local employment and participating in national groups that undercut farm prices. When people are suffering, it is tempting to scapegoat a minority in the community.

People who would oppose hate groups often don't know that they are present in their communities as the groups sometimes operate beneath the radar range of sensitive Christians. Also, actions by hate groups against black farmers and migrant workers seldom make headline news.

The Columbus, Ohio-based Rural Chaplains Association is addressing the growing presence of hate groups in rural communities. The chaplains try to find ways to prevent hate groups from using public facilities to promote their activities. They've learned about laws that safeguard the public from hate activities, and they advocate new laws to protect people from hate crimes.

A basic resource for such action is *When Hate Groups Come to Town: A Handbook for Effective Community Responses* (Center for Democratic Renewal, 1992; available by calling 404-221-0025).

What Can a Local Church Do?

- Ask for a moratorium on locating hazardous waste treatment, storage, and disposal facilities in low-income/people-of-color communities.

- Advocate comprehensive legislation that remedies these injustices and adequately protects all citizens and the environment.

- Become aware of community disposal sites and waste treatment facilities, who is responsible for the production of wastes, and what segment of the community is negatively affected by waste disposal.

Teaching Plan

1. Open with a prayer: "God of all people, we confess that we have given little attention to actions that don't affect our lives. Make us sensitive to decisions made by our community leaders, decisions that adversely affect others who may feel powerless. In the name of Christ, we pray."

2. Discuss: Should special consideration be given to black farmers to compensate for past discriminatory practices?

3. Ask: Where is trash from your backyard taken? Who lives near that landfill?

4. Have the group make a list of things that people tend to fight against having in their neighborhoods (for example, malls, airports, prisons, group homes, cell-phone towers, roads, adult businesses, and stadiums).

5. Roleplay a city council meeting where council members are trying to decide where to locate a hazardous waste facility. Some class members will be members of the council while others assume the roles of middle-class homeowners, upper-class homeowners, and poor homeowners.

Local Action Report

Carol Whitley Key, 69, expressed her concern about foreclosures on family farms by marching with Jesse Jackson to protest the loss of a minority-owned farm near her own farm in rural Trenton, Missouri.

Key has worked with state and national legislators to mitigate the effects of the farm crisis and to reduce the risk of pesticides on imported fruits and vegetables.

In the 1990s, she helped form her area's first citizen's environmental organization to prevent the construction of a hazardous waste facility in northern Missouri. Key and the organization have also worked with the Missouri Department of Natural Resources to ensure that large hog confinement operations do not pollute local water supplies; and they've worked with the Missouri Conservation Department to plant trees and monitor water quality in rivers and streams in the Trenton area.

In 1997, Key helped found the Trenton Master Gardeners, a group that plants and maintains several public gardens in the area, including one at her church, where she helps 9- to 12-year-olds grow vegetables for a food pantry.

A member of Dockery Chapel United Methodist Church, Key has served on various mission teams and formed an environmental group at her church that cleans up 10 miles of roadsides.

Key is the 2001 recipient of the Southern Methodist University's Perkins School of Theology Woodrow B. Seals Laity Award, presented annually to laypersons that exemplify Christian faith and commitment to Christ. (*Interpreter*, July–August 2001)

Section Three

Energy Resources Utilization

SOCIAL PRINCIPLE ¶160B

Affirming the inherent value of nonhuman creation, we support and encourage social policies that are directed toward rational and restrained transformation of parts of the nonhuman world into energy for human usage and that de-emphasize or eliminate energy-producing technologies that endanger the health, the safety, and even the existence of the present and future human and nonhuman creation. Further, we urge wholehearted support of the conservation of energy and responsible development of all energy resources, with special concern for the development of renewable energy sources, that the goodness of the earth may be affirmed.

I hate, I despise your festivals, / and I take no delight in your solemn assemblies. / Even though you offer me your burnt offerings and grain offerings, / I will not accept them; / and your offerings of well-being of your fatted animals / I will not look upon. / Take away from me the noise of your songs; I will not listen to the melody of your harps. / But let justice roll down like waters, / and righteousness like an everflowing stream.—*Amos 5:21-24*

The good leave an inheritance to their children's children.—*Proverbs 13:22*

Chapter 6

Stewards of Spaceship Earth

Core Bible Passages

Psalm 8; Amos 5:24; Matthew 6:25-34; 25:24-28

Humankind enjoys a unique place in God's universe. On the one hand, we are simply one of God's many finite creatures, made from the "dust of the earth," bounded in time and space, fallible in judgment, limited in control, dependent upon our Creator, and interdependent with all other creatures. On the other hand, we are created in the very image of God, with the divine Spirit breathed into us, and entrusted with "dominion" over God's creation (Genesis 1:26, 28; 2:7; Psalm 8:6). We are . . . caretakers with God of the world in which we live."

Two Dangers for the Planet

The 2000 General Conference cited two dangers for humans on this planet.

"The first danger is *arrogance:* that we may overestimate the extent of human control over our environment and the soundness of human judgments concerning it. [In fact, we still know very little about the ecosystem in which we live.] We may underestimate the limits of the planet where we live; and we may understand "dominion" to mean exploitation instead of stewardship.

"The second danger is *irresponsibility:* that we may fail to be the responsible stewards of the earth." We may choose to bury our "talents" while awaiting the Master's return (Matthew 25:24–28). Or we may "demonstrate our faith in God by becoming God's *avant-garde* in "shaping the new human society that will emerge in the twenty-first century. We cannot, therefore, neglect the task of seeking to embody in the world the values that we hold in covenant with God. Nor can we forget the forgiving grace in Jesus Christ, which alone makes us bold enough, or the hope in Christ, which alone keeps us from despair." (From *The Book of Resolutions, 2000*; pages 72–73)

The Values We Seek

General Conference established two values to be sought as we consider any energy policy:

"(1) *Justice.* Ever since the first covenant between God and Israel, and especially since the eighth-century prophets, the people of God have understood that they bear a special concern for justice. 'Let justice roll down like waters, / and righteousness like an everflowing stream' (Amos 5:24) is a cry echoed in hundreds of contexts throughout the Old and New Testaments. Biblical righteousness includes a special concern for the least and the last: the poor, the captive, the oppressed (Luke 4:18; Isaiah 61:1–2). Energy policies that Christians can support, then, will seek to actualize the multifaceted biblical vision of justice. They will be policies that close rather than widen the gap dividing wealth and poverty, rich nations and poor. They will be measures that liberate rather than oppress. They will be programs that distribute fairly the benefits, burdens, and hazards of energy production and consumption, taking into consideration those not yet born as well as the living. They will thus be strategies that give priority to meeting basic human needs such as air, water, food, clothing, and shelter.

"(2) *Sustainability.* Only recently have we humans come to recognize that creation [finitude] entails limits to the resources entrusted to us as stewards of the earth. In particular, we have come up against limits to the nonrenewable fuels available for our consumption and limits to our environment's capacity to absorb poisonous wastes. These double limits mean that humans can betray their stewardship either by using up resources faster than they can be replaced or by releasing wastes in excess of the planet's capacity to absorb them. We now know that humans have the capacity to destroy human life and perhaps even life itself on this planet, and to do so in a very short period of time. Energy policy decisions, therefore, must be measured by sustainability as a criterion in addition to justice. In terms of energy policy, sustainability means energy use that will not: (a) deplete the earth's resources in such a way that our descendants will not be able to continue human society at the level that is adequate for a good quality of life, and (b) pollute the environment to such an extent that human life cannot be sustained in the future. These guidelines for sustainability must include considerations of quality of life as well as mere biological continuance." (From *The Book of Resolutions*; pages 73–74)

Assessing Energy Sources

The United Methodist Church does not expect a return to a world in which people read by candlelight and heat their houses with firewood. However, the denomination wants all energy sources to be calmly assessed in relationship to benefits and costs and then these measures be used in determining choices among energy options.

For example, the large-scale use of our coal resources poses many problems. Underground mining, in addition to operational accidents, causes disabling illness or death from black lung. Strip-mining can despoil an area and ruin it for further use if restoration measures are not practiced. The burning of coal causes large-scale pollution and seriously alters the environment by increasing the carbon dioxide content of the atmosphere, contributing to global warming.

Hydroelectric power also has significant environmental costs. In addition to deaths from industrial accidents, many dam sites are (or were) attractive scenic areas. Destroying (or diminishing) natural beauty areas is objectionable to most of us. Possible dam failure with the resultant flood damage must also be considered in evaluating this energy source.

The use of petroleum products creates severe environmental problems. Tankers and offshore wells create spills and devastate seacoast areas; the damage is long-lasting or permanent. Atmospheric pollution from emissions is far from being under control, especially in dense population centers.

The nuclear energy option also has many problems to be faced. The hazards of storing radioactive wastes for thousands of years and the destructive potential of a catastrophic accident involves a great risk of irreversible damage to the environment and the human genetic pool. (From *The Book of Resolutions, 2000*; pages 74–75).

Solar and wind energy offer promising prospects; yet there is an attendant expense of development. The cost of utilizing these resources will reduce resources needed to meet other human needs. We must face a future in which all persons develop the wise sense to be frugal in the use of any and all resources so that no person is reduced to want of suffering.

Scientists Say Our Future Is in the Balance

In 1992, Sir Michael Atiyah, president of the Royal Society of London, and Dr. Frank Press, president of the United States National Academy of Sciences, issued a joint statement under the title, "Population Growth, Resource Consumption and a Sustainable World." The Royal Society, founded in 1660, is sometimes called the United Kingdom's Academy of Science.

The scientists noted that "developed countries, with 85 percent of the world's gross national product and 23 percent of its population, account for the majority of mineral and fossil-fuel consumption." They warned that efforts by the developing world to achieve living standards based on the same levels of consumption as the developed world could lead to catastrophic outcomes for the global environment.

They declared that the "application of science and technology to global problems is a key component to providing a decent standard of living for a majority of the human race." The group said science and technology can help developing countries effectively manage their resources and allow them to "participate fully in worldwide initiatives for common benefit."

The scientists want to strengthen capabilities in science and technology in less developed nations. They also warn that "science and technology alone are not enough. Global policies are urgently needed to promote more rapid economic development throughout the world, more environmentally benign patterns of human activity, and a more rapid stabilization of world population."

They concluded, "The future of our planet is in the balance. Sustainable development can be achieved, but only if irreversible degradation of the environment can be halted in time. The next 30 years may be crucial."

Clean Up Your Room

Churches are generally unaware of the extent to which persons are either prevented from being in church facilities by pollutants or endure them only at considerable personal discomfort or illness.

Sources of indoor pollution in church buildings include chemical fumes from gas stoves and furnaces, pesticides, cleaning materials, formaldehyde, candles, paint, photocopy machines, restroom deodorizers, and radon as well as particulates such as dust, mold, and asbestos fibers.

Additional pollutants are brought into church buildings in the form of perfume, cologne, and other scents; dry-cleaning odors; and cigarette smoke (which itself releases over 1,000 chemicals into the air).

The problem in church buildings is compounded by

(a) the general absence of effective air circulation systems that can mechanically circulate fresh air, and

(b) improved insulating of buildings in recent decades, which, while conserving heat, also reduces the rate of air exchange and allows the buildup of concentration of the indoor pollution. United States government studies have shown indoor air pollution levels to be as much as eight times higher than outdoor air pollution.

Indoor air pollution is not only a problem for those who are allergic or otherwise sensitive to indoor pollution. The long-term effects of such pollution could potentially be detrimental to anyone. Modern living conditions expose the human body to an incredible level of chemical exposure, for which the long-term effects are only partially known. Lung cancer and other sickness resulting from exposure to smoke, whether to smokers themselves or to involuntary smokers exposed to sidestream smoke, are the most widely publicized of the potential long-term effects on everyone.

There is much that churches and church institutions can do to minimize the effect of indoor air pollution. Some churches have already taken steps to reduce indoor air pollution and to address the needs of those seriously affected. (From *The Book of Resolutions, 1996;* pages 81–82)

What Can a Local Church Do?

- Advocate a strenuous national effort to conserve energy that includes insulation, co-generation, recycling, public transportation, more efficient motors in appliances and engines in automobiles as well as the elimination of waste and a more simplified lifestyle. The technology for such steps is already known and commercially available; it requires only dissemination of information and stronger public support, including larger tax incentives than are presently available.

■ Become a model for energy conservation by doing such things as installing dampers in furnaces, insulating adequately all church properties, heating and lighting only rooms that are in use, using air circulation, and exploring alternative energy sources such as solar energy.

■ Urge members to assess their own energy consumption, find ways to conserve, to eliminate waste, to revise transportation patterns, and to simplify lifestyles as a model for sound stewardship of the limited resources.

■ Advocate increased government funding for research and development of renewable energy sources, especially solar energy, and government incentives to speed the application of the resulting technologies to energy needs, wherever appropriate. The greatest national effort should be made in the areas of conservation and renewable energy sources.

■ Oppose any national energy policy that will result in continuing exploitation of Native Americans. The despoiling of Native American lands and the increased health problems that have resulted among Native Americans because of the mining of coal and the milling of uranium must cease.

■ Oppose any national energy program that increases the financial burden on the poor, the elderly, and those with fixed incomes. Churches should advocate legislation that will cushion the impact of higher energy prices on the poor.

■ Engage in a serious study of energy issues in the context of Christian faith and the values of justice and sustainability. (From *The Book of Resolutions, 2000*; pages 75–76)

■ Join the Environmental Justice Network of the General Board of Church and Society (Web page: *http://www.umc-gbcs.org/ej_network.htm*). The network addresses a wide variety of environmental issues, including climate change, energy policy, toxics, environmental health, endangered species, environmental racism and classism, sustainable communities, consumption, agriculture, and genetics. Members of the Network receive a quarterly newsletter and action alerts and background information on US public policy and legislative issues.

- Complete an energy audit of the congregation's environmental practices. What kinds of plates and cups are used? How energy efficient is the heating and air conditioning system? Is the insulation adequate? What temperatures are maintained? Develop an action plan to reduce energy consumption and seek support of the church council to implement the plan. An energy guide is available at *http://www.epa.gov/smallbiz/doc/ congregations.pdf.*

- Urge church members to participate in "environmental tithing." Tithers reduce their burden on the earth's bounty by producing ten percent less waste, consuming ten percent less of nonrenewable resources, and contributing the savings to environmental causes.

Teaching Plan

1. Open with a prayer: "God of all creation, we care about our world. We want to be good stewards of creation, but we often feel confused or powerless. Open our minds and hearts to new ideas. Give us a renewed sense of hope. Show us what we can do each day to care for our earth; in Christ's name we pray."

2. Read aloud Psalm 8 and Matthew 6:25-34. Ask: What does Scripture have to say about humanity's place within creation? What kind of life do the passages envision?

3. Read aloud Amos 5:21–24. Ask: What solemn assemblies do we hold that would bring no delight to God? What actions should we take that would enable "justice to roll down like waters"?

4. Develop a checklist for items that should be used in making an inventory of your church's environmental practices. (To view a church energy audit, see *http://www.epa.gov/smallbiz/doc/congregations.pdf.*)

Local Action Report

Nina Nichols attended Glen Lake Camp in Glen Rose, Texas, for the first time when she was in the fourth grade; she's been spending her summers there ever since. Now an ordained United Methodist minister, Nichols recalls the time she first applied to work on Glen Lake's summer staff.

"I was a rebellious young college student," she reports, "with half my hair shaved off over one ear. I felt it was one reason they hired me—to help reach kids on the periphery."

Sure enough, one 15-year-old boy with a Mohawk haircut asked her to buy cigarettes for him. *After all, with all her energy and unorthodox hairdo,* he thought, *she just had to be on drugs.* "No," she told him, "I'm high on life."

Over the next few years, the boy continued to attend Glen Lake. One day he volunteered to help her clean up the river and told her he had quit using drugs.

Members of the Glen Lake Camp frequently engage in environmental ministries such as planting trees. (*Interpreter*, July-August, 1998; page 15)

The North Oxnard United Methodist Church is located in a coastal area of California. After conducting an energy audit, the congregation launched an energy-saving program in which they saved $2,600 in the first year.

Due to a mild climate, lighting enhancements became the major focus for the small congregation. Members replaced inefficient incandescent lights with new fluorescent reflector-type lamps. When light output was reduced, the congregation slightly modified the fixtures to alter light distribution and enhance visual comfort.

Members also fixed leaky faucets and replaced a leaky old seven-gallon-per-flush toilet with an efficient 1.6-gallon-per-flush unit. They then removed two old inefficient refrigerators with newer models.

The church's ongoing water- and energy-efficiency program allowed the congregation to take a leadership role in encouraging other churches in the California-Pacific Conference to participate in similar energy-saving actions.

Chapter 7

Paper or Plastic?

Core Bible Passages

Psalm 8; Matthew 6:25-34; 25:24-28

Weary from a long day at work, Roger shuffles through the aisles of the grocery store. He tries to make choices that meet his shopping needs and that are environmentally friendly. He chooses nonaerosal hairspray; toilet tissue and paper towels made from recycled paper; frozen foods with just one layer of packaging; and concentrated laundry detergent, because the size of the cardboard box is smaller.

Then he pauses at the disposable cups. Should he buy paper or Styrofoam? One comes from trees, the other from oil. Martin B. Hocking, writing in *Science*, acknowledges the complexity of the choice and makes a case for polystyrene over paper. The main raw material for paper cups is wood, a renewable resource; however, the acquisition of wood for making pulp mars the landscape with road accesses and clear-cutting. In a watershed area, extensive clear-cutting increases maximum flows and decreases minimum flows of streams. The likelihood of flood and drought increases in such areas. The article asserts that the impact of producing the polystyrene cup made from hydrocarbons (oil and gas) is significant, yet less than that of producing paper cups. Producing the paper cup requires about twelve times as much steam, thirty-six times as much electricity, and twice as much cooling water as the polystyrene cup. This increase is reflected in the price: paper cups cost about two and one half times more than polystyrene cups.

American City and County magazine also reports the benefits of recycling polystyrene. Recycled foam can be used in many products such as egg cartons, videotapes, and insulation. On the other hand, polystyrene is not biodegradable.

In the end, Roger decides not to purchase disposable cups because he cannot decide whether paper or Styrofoam is better. He waits in line, looks at the magazines in the stands, and wonders how many trees it takes to create all that paper. A cheery voice breaks his depressed reverie and forces him to make yet one more environmentally conscious choice, "Paper or plastic?" Roger's mouth drops open. Which one? Does it really matter?

What Can a Local Church Do?

- Purchase trash cans for a park or recreation area.

- Befriend a highway by cleaning up litter.

- Collect Christmas trees for recycling.

- Collect telephone books, newspapers, and aluminum cans for recycling.

- Start an "issues alert phone tree" to inform people about issues being debated in Congress or the state legislature.

Teaching Plan

1. Spend a minute in silence. Become attentive to signs of the natural world in your midst. Then pray together the following: "God of all creation, we care about our world. We want to be good stewards of creation, but we often feel confused or powerless. Open our minds and hearts to new ideas. Give us a renewed sense of hope. Show us what we can do each day to care for our earth; in the name of Christ we pray."

2. Read the story of Roger at the beginning of this chapter. Have your group form two or three teams. Tell the teams to imagine that they are grocery shopping. Have them name the products that make them stop and think about environmental issues. If you have time, you may have them create and present a brief skit about their experiences.

3. Debate the use of paper plates for church suppers. Consider cost of hot water, wear and tear on dishwashing equipment, time spent by volunteers, cost of manufacturing paper, cost of hauling trash, and use of landfills.

4. Form teams. Give each team a simple item such as a T-shirt, a bag of sugar, or a small appliance. Ask the groups to trace what had to happen in order for its item to be produced, manufactured, transported, obtained, and used by a consumer. Remember to include all hidden costs such as electricity or wash water.

5. Worship. Make an altar in the center of the learning area and place a candle, a Bible, a small paper bag, and a small plastic bag on it. Give each participant paper and pencil. Invite them to write a brief, personal psalm that expresses praise to God, gratitude for creation, and a renewed sense of our role as God's steward of creation. Use Psalm 8 as a model.

Local Action Report

Inspired by numerous sermons on preserving God's earth, members of First United Methodist Church in Ypsilanti, Michigan, became an "Earth Covenant Church," a program sponsored by the Detroit Annual Conference's Environmental Justice Division.

"Our commitment to the earth is much needed in today's world," says Edith Hurst, who serves as the environmental coordinator for the 500-member congregation. "By helping to care for all of creation, our church is aiding in the fulfillment of the reign of God on the earth."

United Methodist Women lead the church in using only permanent dinnerware. Cans, aluminum, paper, plastic, and cardboard are recycled; and office staff buy recycled supplies and send church newsletters through e-mail to conserve paper.

Church trustees make sure the church and parsonage are energy efficient; and the janitors use environmentally friendly materials and have stopped using snow blowers and salt on the sidewalks.

In addition, members write letters to legislators about environmental issues, support the rain forest, have "adopted" several streets, and have designated April as "Earth Month." (*Interpreter*, July–August, 1998; page 18)

Living in the natural beauty of western Michigan, Jenny Frye became concerned about the growing trash mountains in Berrien County. Her first actions involved her own household and teaching her three young children proper respect for the environment. She began composting kitchen and yard waste for use in her garden. She separated and recycled paper, glass, plastic, and tin cans. Then Jenny became concerned about the example being set for her children by her own church.

Peace Temple, like many other United Methodist congregations, always held a coffee fellowship between the Sunday morning worship service and Sunday school. Adults drank their coffee or tea from Styrofoam cups. The children drank their fruit punch from paper cups. After the coffee fellowship, all the cups went in the trash. It was convenient. Jenny believed that serving convenience is never enough. She was determined to see if she could make a difference. She proposed to the administrative council that a ban be placed on the use of disposable cups at Peace Temple.

Since volunteers prepared the coffee each Sunday, an immediate objection was raised to the proposed ban. Who would wash the crockery if the new policy were initiated? It was enough to ask volunteers to prepare coffee each week. Asking volunteers to wash dishes after the coffee fellowship was just too much. Maybe it was easier to continue using the disposable cups.

As often happens at church meetings, a council member had another idea. Why not put up a mug rack like he had seen at some neighborhood restaurants? Everybody could have his or her own mug. People could bring their own mug from their home for use each Sunday. In a few weeks the rack was in place. Each member seemed to outdo the other in selecting a zany mug to place on the rack. Of course, a few sensible mugs were always in place for visitors. After each use, everybody would rinse his or her mug and place it back on the rack.

The mug rack became a hit; besides, coffee and tea always taste better when drunk from a real mug. Members could see their mug on the rack; it was always there inviting them back next Sunday. The use of a personal mug deepened the sense of fellowship and solved the solid-waste problem at the same time.

Then Jenny suggested that the coffee grounds did not need to be placed in the garbage can. The coffee grounds soon became mulch around the rose bushes at the church and parsonage.

Section Four

✓ Animal Life

SOCIAL PRINCIPLE ¶160C

We support regulations that protect the life and health of animals, including those ensuring the humane treatment of pets and other domestic animals, animals used in research, and the painless slaughtering of meat animals, fish, and fowl. We encourage the preservation of all animal species including those threatened with extinction.

And of every living thing of all flesh, you shall bring two of every kind into the ark, to keep them alive with you; they shall be male and female. Of the birds according to their kinds, and of the animals according to their kinds, of every creeping thing of the ground according to its kind, two of every kind shall come in to you, to keep them alive.—*Genesis 6:19-20*

The clever see danger and hide; / but the simple go on, and suffer for it.—*Proverbs 22:3*

Chapter 8

Thrown Off the Ark

Core Bible Passages

Genesis 6:5–8:22

Noah was instructed to keep the animals, birds, and every living thing "alive with [him]." It appears that we've engaged in the routine practice of throwing a variety of these creatures off our ark. *The Environment* (Abingdon, 1994; page 16) reports that the rate of extinction for plant and animal species has increased from one each 190 years to one every twenty minutes.

In the last 400 years, many kinds of wildlife have become extinct. In North America, such species include the Carolina parakeet, the passenger pigeon, the California grizzly bear, and a birch that once grew in Virginia. Beginning in the late 1800s, growing concern for the world's vanishing wildlife has led to increased conservation action. Governments of many nations have passed protective laws and set aside national parks and other reserves for wildlife. Such efforts have saved the American bison, the pronghorn antelope, and many of the rare plants found on the Hawaiian and Galapagos Islands.

But several hundred species of animals and thousands of species of plants presently face extinction. Such animals include the Asiatic lion, the Bengal tiger, the blue whale, the mountain gorilla, the whooping crane, the California condor, and all the Asian rhinoceroses. Plants that are facing extinction include the black cabbage tree, the Ozark chestnut, the St. Helena redwood, and several kinds of California manzanitas.

Three main classifications are commonly used for animals and plants at risk: (1) endangered, (2) vulnerable, and (3) lower risk.

The California condor is endangered because only about 170 birds of this species still exist, most of them in captivity. In 1987, wildlife biologists captured what was then the last remaining wild California condor. Since then, more than 100 California condors have been hatched and raised in captivity. Scientists have released some of these birds into the wild in California and Arizona.

Vulnerable species, also known as threatened species, may be abundant in some areas, but they face serious dangers nevertheless. These dangers may result from unfavorable changes in the environment. They also may be due to extensive hunting, fishing, or trapping, or even collecting by hobbyists. The gray wolf, a vulnerable species, is plentiful in some places; but its overall numbers worldwide are threatened by hunting, trapping, and poisoning.

Lower risk species, also known as rare species, have small populations. They often live in restricted geographical areas, but their numbers are not necessarily decreasing. For example, the rare bristlecone pine trees grow only at high altitudes in the Western United States; but their survival is not seriously threatened.

Recent Efforts to Conserve Endangered Species

Since the late 1900s, a different kind of conservation philosophy has begun to emerge. Many environmentalists and philosophers now believe that nonhuman species have inherent rights of existence. This movement, foreshadowed in the writings of Henry David Thoreau and John Muir, seeks to give conservation a deeper respect for nature and to make such respect the cornerstone of conservation laws (*2001 World Book Encyclopedia*).

In 1993, the Office on Environmental Policy was established. It coordinates environmental policy within the federal government. Such policy increasingly attempts to manage entire ecosystems for the benefit of all the species within them, rather than producing individual management plans for each species as it becomes threatened.

Jobs Versus Species Preservation

"Imagine you live in a community that has the last known spawning area for a fish that has been classified as endangered. For several years a resource management team has worked to save and to improve the environmental quality. . . ." Environmental groups from around the world applaud these efforts. "From the beginning, each step of your community's habitat-restoration effort has been documented as part of a long-term university research project.

"The future of this project is threatened by a recent event in your community. An entertainment company that is the second largest employer in the area announces expansion plans that will destroy the spawning area. They argue that this facility will produce many jobs. Furthermore, the company is asking the local government to support this expansion through tax incentives and government insured low-interest loans.

"Your community is [rather evenly] split between the two sides in this dispute. Company representatives contend that a hearing is not needed because the fish has no commercial value. Project supporters produce a bumper sticker that reads, 'Eat Fish, Save Jobs!'

"Those who oppose the project maintain that any loss of jobs will be minimal compared to those which will result from internal management decisions of the entertainment company. These jobs will be lost due to increases in efficiency as the company reorganizes its staffing configuration and becomes more automated. A local newspaper has obtained a copy of a company memo marked 'Confidential' that supports this contention. Company officials have confirmed the existence of the memo, but they contend that its contents are being taken out of context. All parties accept that there will be numerous court battles before the matter is resolved.

"By holding a hearing, your local government is attempting to collect information that will be evaluated before a final decision is made on whether or not to support this expansion project.

"This hearing will include representatives from the habitat-restoration effort, the entertainment company proposing the project, and the local government."

(From *The Environment*, by Larry Dunlap Berg; Abingdon, 1994; page 19)

You will have the chance to speak at the public library. What will be your position? What information will you need to be persuasive? Will facts matter, or is the "fix" already in? What difference will it make if the spawning area is lost? Can an alternative spawning area be developed? What is gained if the fish species is preserved? What is lost if the species disappears? How can the need for jobs be balanced with the requirements of conservation? Is the choice even a "either/or" decision?

What Can a Local Church Do?

- Help at the local animal shelter.

- Advocate for humane conditions for livestock.

- Offer workshops to teach children how to care for pets.

- Monitor legislative proposals and zoning decisions that could affect wildlife.

- Post literature on animal rights on the church bulletin board.

Teaching Plan

1. Pray together: "O God, you have given life to an abundance of animals, insects, and plants, and we confess that we have not understood our role in protecting these life forms. Help us to know what we can do to be better stewards of this planet. In the name of Christ we pray."

2. Sing or read together "God of the Sparrow God of the Whale" (*The United Methodist Hymnal*, 122). Then ask: What does it mean to you to think of being just one part of the whole of creation that responds to God? How does the human response differ from that of the sparrow or whale?

3. Discuss how the value of a species is determined. Is the species of value because it is a future source of food, medicine, or other product? Is it of value because of its size or its beauty?

4. Roleplay. Read "Jobs Versus Species Protection" on pages 64–65. Then have class members roleplay the environmentalist, leaders of the entertainment company, unemployed workers, and members of the city council.

Local Action Report

Venture Crew, a group of young people from Clear Branch United Methodist Church in Trussville, Alabama, paddled canoes through several central Alabama rivers in order to produce a multimedia presentation for schools and other organizations showing the environmental problems that exist. The group, ages 14 to 21, wanted to motivate others to help "mind the rivers." The group received a $5,000 grant from the United States Environmental Protection Agency.

Space

SOCIAL PRINCIPLE ¶160D

The universe, known and unknown, is the creation of God and is due the respect we are called to give the earth.

When I look at your heavens, / the work of thy fingers, / the moon and the stars that you have established; / what are human beings that you are mindful of them, / mortals that you care for them? / Yet you have made them a little lower than God, / and crowned them with glory and honor. / You have given them dominion over the works of your hands; / you have put all things under their feet, / all sheep and oxen, and also the beasts of the field, / the birds of the air, and the fish of the sea, / whatever passes along the paths of the seas.—*Psalm 8:3–8*

Where is the way to the dwelling of light, / and where is the place of darkness, / that you may take it to its territory / and that you may discern the paths to its home?—*Job 38:19–20*

Chapter 9

Faith in Space

Core Bible Passages

Joshua 10:6–14; Job 38; Revelation 6:12–17

The heavens once provoked wonder. People steered themselves across vast oceans and found their way to freedom just by following the stars. Scientific martyrs lost their lives by challenging popular ideas about what lay "beyond." For many, it was God's own self who dwelt above, and we raised our hands and hearts to heaven.

In July 1969, humanity dared to step upon the face of the moon. President Richard Nixon called it "the greatest week in the history of the world since the Creation." The American public, who watched on their television sets as the astronauts took one large step for humankind, agreed.

Today, we continue to find new wonders about space; but some of the awe seems to be missing.

A Brief History

Although it is sometimes difficult to believe, the history of the United States space program was born less than 50 years ago in October 1958. At this time, jet passenger service was still a novelty. The Russians had launched Sputnik, the first artificial satellite. According to the White House, Sputnik "created a crisis of confidence that swept the country like a windblown forest fire." The idea of landing on the moon still lay in the realm of science fiction, but the escalating Cold War required a comprehensive and bold response. The National Aeronautics and Space Administration (NASA) was created. What was its mission? To pioneer the future.

With the Mercury, Gemini, and Apollo missions, NASA succeeded in supplying a Cold War victory by delivering the moon's first footprints to the United States. Its scientists never stopped dreaming. In April 1981, the world's first reusable spacecraft, the space shuttle *Columbia*, was launched and 54 hours later returned successfully to earth. Other NASA spacecraft using cameras and remote sensing instruments have visited every planet in the solar system except little Pluto (which is now not even considered a planet by many scientists). On Independence Day in 1997, Sojourner, a robot rover the size of a child's Tonka truck, roamed around the surface of Mars, sending photographs back to earth as part of the Pathfinder mission. This mission reflected NASA's new philosophy of "faster, cheaper, better," and cost only $270 million, just a few dollars more than the price tag of the movie *Titanic*.

There is also the $1.5 billion Hubble Space Telescope, launched in April 1990 on a 15-year mission as a cosmic tourist sending back snapshots of the universe. To date, the Hubble has captured hundreds of images, including the blaze surrounding a family of stars being born two hundred thousand light years away and a planet outside our solar system that was spotted hurtling though space at 20,000 miles per hour. Scientists and school children alike can examine these images as they are displayed in a variety of sites on the World Wide Web. These are just a prologue. A flip through any newspaper will reveal many other discoveries that no longer receive front-page coverage. These achievements seem only a prologue to the possibilities that await.

The Big Bang

Not all the exploration and discovery of the heavens today is being done in spacecraft. Throughout the scientific community, physics and abstract thought are being used to develop theories that explain our universe. Today most scientists believe two things to be true: (1) we live in an expanding universe that is approximately 15 billion years old, and (2) our sun will burn itself out in 5 billion years. Many others are united around the belief of a "big bang" in which all the material in the universe was packed into one location and exploded outward, creating the space of our universe and the far-flung galaxies that inhabit it. Some scientists, such as Steven Hawking, have speculated that the originating condition of the universe leaves no room for outside influences and, therefore, that of a divine creator. "What place then, for a creator?" he asks. Others look at the theory and see affirmation of the Christian idea of God's creation as *ex nihilo* ("out of nothing").

Amid the scientific debate, however, there seems to be a noticeable absence of theologians' voices. The United Methodist Church, for instance, has only one sentence in the Social Principles regarding space.

Many church officials suggest that science, not faith, is providing us our theological ideas of God and creation. For many of us, God gets relegated to the dark corners of life, where the light of science has not yet shone.

To address this matter, a number of groups are forming partnerships between scientific and religious minds; books such as *Science and Theology: The New Consonance* are beginning to pour into book stores; and Public Television has produced a documentary on faith and science. But in many cases, this melding of God and what can be viewed in the telescope has yet to filter down into everyday lives.

Earth is "a medium-sized planet orbiting around an average star in the outer suburbs of an ordinary spiral galaxy, which is itself only one of about a million million galaxies in the observable universe"—Stephen Hawking

"Somewhere, something incredible is waiting to be known." —Carl Sagan

"Where were you when I laid the foundation of the earth? Tell me if you have understanding. / Who determined its measurements—surely you know."— Job 38:4–5

Teaching Plan

1. Worship. Sing the first stanza of "How Great Thou Art." Ask: What do you think of when you sing about the "worlds" God has made? Turn off the lights to darken the room or have participants close their eyes as they sing the hymn again, imagining the far reaches of space as they sing.

2. Ask: Where were you when astronauts took the first steps on the moon? Do any of the other space-related events resonate in your personal life?

3. Study psalms. Read Psalms 19:1–6; 84:11; 104:1–4; 147:4; and 148:1–6. Ask: What do these songs reveal about the character of God? Form small groups and ask the groups to write a psalm that expresses their ideas about the character and attributes of God.

4. Imagine. Ask the class to cast themselves back in history and imagine that they have been chosen to decide the fate of Galileo. Do his statements about an earth that rotates about a sun threaten your faith?

5. Consider current problems related to terrorism, hunger, and poverty. Ask: Should we still be spending money on a space program?

Scientists continue to search for intelligent life in other places in the universe. How would the discovery of an alien life form affect your faith?

6. Space and Faith. The United Methodist Church's statement on space and faith (page 69) is very brief. Ask: Should the church say more? Compose a statement that addresses the concerns of people of faith about space exploration.

Local Action Report

Lake Merritt United Methodist Church in Oakland, California, sponsored a spring camp for young people titled "Go Galactic!—An Outer Space Experience."

The weeklong event in April enabled students to study the solar system. Through hands-on projects, films, and experiments, students learned about the origin of the universe and our neighboring planets as well as how gravity works. A classroom planetarium demonstrated the day and night cycles, the seasons on earth, and the phases of the moon.

Some of the hands-on projects included

- A planet mobile
- Rockets
- Satellites
- A flying comet toy
- Gravity toys
- Outer space aliens

Section Six

Science and Technology

SOCIAL PRINCIPLE ¶160E

We recognize science as a legitimate interpretation of God's natural world. We affirm the validity of the claims of science in describing the natural world, although we preclude science from making authoritative claims about theological issues. We recognize technology as a legitimate use of God's natural world when such use enhances human life and enables all of God's children to develop their God-given creative potential without violating our ethical convictions about the relationship of humanity to the natural world.

In acknowledging the important roles of science and technology, however, we also believe that theological understandings of human experience are crucial to a full understanding of the place of humanity in the universe. Science and theology are complementary rather than mutually incompatible. We therefore encourage dialogue between the scientific and theological communities and seek the kind of participation that will enable humanity to sustain life on earth and, by God's grace, increase the quality of our common lives together.

Anyone who claims to know something does not yet have the necessary knowledge.—*1 Corinthians 8:2*

Brothers and sisters, do not be children in your thinking; rather, be infants in evil, but in thinking be adults.—*1 Corinthians 14:20*

See to it that no one takes you captive through philosophy and empty deceit, according to human tradition according to the elemental spirits of the universe, and not according to Christ.—*Colossians 2:8*

Test everything; hold fast to what is good; abstain from every form of evil.—*1 Thessalonians 5:21-22*

Chapter 10

The **Great Debate**

Core Bible Passages

Romans 1:18–23; Acts 17:16–34; Colossians 1:15–20

What is the relationship between science and faith? The long dialogue has been fraught with heat and sometimes with light. Some would say that they proceed from two different starting points, that science starts the answer with the questions of what, how, when, and where; faith seeks to answer why, who, and to what purpose.

John Callahan, author of *Science and Christianity*, says the Bible is the greatest book ever written. It contains the writings of great men of God who were largely inspired by him. However, as any other document, it is not absolutely perfect, and in some places it is badly flawed. The Bible, he says, can be used as evidence to help us understand reality, but reality cannot be defined by the Bible. Observation and experimentation in addition to divine revelation are the keys humanity uses to unlock the secrets of the universe.

Callahan notes the staggering dimensions of the universe with a hundred billion stars in our galaxy alone, and there are 100 billion other galaxies. He notes the age of the earth (4.5 billion years) and the evolution of a variety of plants and animals. But, he says, none of this information changes his belief that God came in the form of the man Jesus Christ, and that Jesus died upon the cross to save us.

Underscoring the view that faith and science are complementary is a 1992 speech by Pope John Paul II that sought to restore Galileo's standing within the Roman Catholic Church. The Pope said, "In 1633, the Vatican put the astronomer under house arrest for writing, against church orders, that the earth revolves around the sun. . . . In the 17th century, theologians failed to distinguish between belief in the Bible and the interpretation of it. Galileo contended that the Scriptures cannot err but are often misunderstood. This insight . . . made the scientist a wiser theologian than his Vatican accusers." (*Time*, December 28, 1992)

An unspoken question in any debate about science and religion is whether either side can prove or disprove the existence of God. Some find evidence of God's handiwork in science, and others find only evidence of a mechanized universe. Some will say that Scriptures prove the existence of God, and others will find them evidence of humankind's feeble attempts to explain the inexplicable.

United Methodists use a quadrilateral form of theological reflection. They use the Bible as a primary document of faith, but they also consider their intellectual capacity (reason), the experience of the church over the ages (tradition), and their lifetime of observations (experience) as necessary grist for the theological mill. Within the quadrilateral, science can be a legitimate partner in the quest for truth, but not the final arbiter of religious truth.

Faith Confronts Reason

Romans 1:18–23. Paul confronts the church at Rome on those things that separate us from God and each other. Paul teaches that God's righteousness is set against the human tendency toward immorality and idolatry—spiritual, material, or even scientific. Paul explains that God's truth is and has always been available to us. Science can help us apprehend knowledge of God by grasping God's nature made manifest in the order and grandeur of God's creation.

Acts 17:16–34. Paul encounters in Athens "wise ones"—philosphers who debate from the basis of observation and logic. Paul points them to the Creation and to the knowable God who created it, reinterpreting a local statue inscription, "To an unknown god." It is this God who has created the natural laws that form the foundation of their arguments.

Colossians 1:15–20. Paul writes to a church disturbed by itinerant philosophers who advocated that trust in Christ for salvation was insufficient, and that other astral powers needed to be satisfied as well. Paul stresses the uniqueness of Christ as the image of God as well as God's agent in the birthing of Creation. All powers are subject to his lordship, and the goal of the created order is to be united in Christ.

Teaching Plan

*1. **Lead the responsive reading of Psalm 8*** (*The United Methodist Hymnal*, 743). Reflect briefly on the ways we see God revealed in the majesty of the creation.

*2. **Consider science and faith.*** On a chalkboard or a large sheet of paper, have the participants list some of the recent scientific discoveries or applications they feel conflict with their faith stance. You might suggest some issue such as genetic engineering or artificial extension of life, which pose moral and ethical dilemmas for many Christians.

*3. **Bible study.*** Read "Faith Confronts Reason" (page 77). Form three groups. Ask each group to consider one of the biblical passages. Ask: Can you think of any current situation similar to those described in these texts?

*4. **More Bible study.*** Have a volunteer read aloud Acts 17:16-34. Then ask participants to consider the essentials of Paul's arguments to the Athenians. Ask them to rephrase Paul's arguments if they were to use them in conversation with the proponents of science today.

*5. **The claims of science.*** One potential problem of science is in overstepping its boundaries; such self-confidence occasionally leads to making claims that cannot be substantiated, regardless of the safeguards of scientific method. One consequence is the elevation of science to idolatrous heights. Discuss how group members might respond, either individually or corporately to the far-reaching claims of science.

*6. **Present agree/disagree statements*** and ask participants to explain their stance:

- Scientific inquiry and religious faith can be friends rather than foes. It takes a certain kind of "faith" to be a scientist.

- Most scientists do not believe in God.

- Scientific information can prove that God does not exist.

- If there is no other life in the universe, then it sure is a waste of space.

- God's existence can be proved.

- Scientific inquiry cannot destroy religious faith but can actually deepen faith.

Local Action Report

Jamie Foster, the choir director of the First United Methodist Church of Arroyo Grande, California, teaches a course entitled "Is God Expanding, Too?"

In eight 90-minute sessions, Foster explores the creation of the universe, the laws of physics, and God's role in both. Foster asks questions such as the following: What are the theories and data of religion, and what are the traditions and judgments of science? What role does revelation play, either on the road to Damascus (Paul) or Bowes Moor (Fred Hoyle)? Does the universe need a creator? Does design imply a designer?

"Participants go away with some marvelous thoughts, ideas, and questions to ponder," reports Foster.

Section Seven

Food Safety

SOCIAL PRINCIPLE ¶160F

W e support policies that protect the food supply and that ensure the public's right to know the content of the foods they are eating. We call for rigorous inspections and controls on the biological safety of all foodstuffs intended for human consumption. We urge independent testing for chemical residues in food, and the removal from the market of foods contaminated with potentially hazardous levels of pesticides, herbicides, or fungicides; drug residues from animal antibiotics, steroids, or hormones; contaminants due to pollution that are carried by air, soil, or water from incinerator plants or other industrial operations. We call for clear labeling of all processed or altered foods, with pre-market safety testing required. We oppose weakening the standards for organic foods. We call for policies that encourage and support a gradual transition to sustainable and organic agriculture.

Salt is good; but if salt has lost its taste, how shall its saltiness be restored? It is fit neither for the soil nor for the manure pile; they throw it away.—*Luke 14:34-35*

Do we not have the right to our food and drink?—*1 Corinthians 9:4*

Chapter 11

How Safe Is Our Food?

Core Bible Passages

Leviticus 11:1-47; Deuteronomy 14:3–21; Luke 14:16-24; Acts 10:9-33; 1 Corinthians 8:1-13

Diseases caused by food in the United States are responsible for an estimated 76 million cases of gastrointestinal illnesses, 325,000 illnesses resulting in hospitalizations, and 5,000 deaths each year, according to the Centers for Disease Control and Prevention.

In a recent interview, Joseph A. Levitt, director of the Food and Drug Administration Center for Food Safety and Applied Nutrition, said the world of food safety has fundamentally changed in many ways. He observes we are now eating a greater variety of foods, particularly seafood and fresh fruits and vegetables that are eaten raw. While he suggests these products may be nutritious, they can also introduce many more sources of potential contamination since they are not cooked.

Levitt further notes there are many kinds of harmful bacteria that can contaminate our food. Americans get their food from all around the world every month of the year. They also eat more food prepared outside the home where more and more food workers become involved in preparing, cooking, and serving the food. So when food is contaminated, there are many more people who are more susceptible to food-borne illness.

An estimated 6 million to 7 million Americans have food allergies, and about 150 people die each year in the United States from severe allergic reactions to food. Dr. Levitt says about 90 percent of these food allergies are attributed to eight types of food: milk, eggs, fish, wheat, tree nuts, peanuts, soybeans, and crustaceans, such as shrimp and crab. It is extremely important for the Food and Drug Administration (FDA) to make certain that all contents of any products are included on the label. That agency produces a Compliance Policy Guide that articulates a simple rule on food allergens for the industry: Because there is a potential for allergic reaction to any ingredient, consumers need to have all ingredients listed on food products.

We now have a food supply that has within it a whole different dynamic than the one with which many people grew up. Does that mean that people need to be afraid? No. What it does mean is that people need to take proper precautions just as they do when they get into their cars and fasten their seatbelts. The FDA reminds all persons preparing food to observe the following practices:

■ Wash hands before preparing food.

■ Keep all cooking services clean.

■ Maintain food at proper hot and cold temperatures.

■ Do not permit raw meat products to cross-contaminate other foods (for example, cutting lettuce on the same surface used to cut raw chicken).

(*FDA Consumer,* September–October 2001)

Food and the Bible

Food plays an important role in the Bible from the promises of God in Genesis to the marriage feast of the Lord in Revelation.

In Genesis 1:29, God gives to Adam and Eve "every plant yielding seed that is upon the face of all the earth, and every tree with seed in its fruit" for food.

Jude 12 condemns the false teachers who taint the love feasts of the Christians. From the original gift of food to ensure life to the agape meals of the early Christian communities that celebrated the hope of eternal life, food weaves in and out of the life and teachings of Scripture.

In Bible lands, the everyday diet consisted of cereals (wheat and barley), legumes, lentils, and dairy products. They also ate such things as olives, grapes, figs, dates, and almonds. Meat, except for the very wealthy, was not a regular part of the diet. Whenever meat was eaten, it was a special occasion, usually in the context of a religious feast or festival. Fish was consumed in those areas where it was available. Because swine are not ruminants and thus could not survive on grasses, pork was forbidden in Jewish life. Swine compete with humans for food; ruminants live on grasses that humans cannot digest.

Spiritually, food was seen as God's gift (Deuteronomy 8:7-10 and 1 Timothy 4:3). It would also be one of the blessings of the age to come (Ezekiel 47:6-12). In John 6:25-34, Jesus compares the eternal food he has to offer with the perishable manna of the Exodus.

Genetically Engineered Food

Even if people purchase only organic produce, they can't be certain that nothing genetically engineered is included because there is no law requiring anyone in the food chain who adds a genetically engineered component to label the seed, plant, or produce as containing genetically altered elements. No law requires the label "This food has been genetically altered." So when people buy potatoes they might be getting potatoes with a fish gene added to increase the shelf life, or a pork gene added to provide firmer flesh.

A 1999 survey found that one-fourth of United States farmland was planted with genetically engineered seeds, which are seeds created by splicing plant or animal genes with particular traits into the DNA of other organisms. According to *Consumer Reports*, 35 percent of all corn, 50 percent of cotton, and 55 percent of soybeans grown in the United States in 1999 were genetically altered. (*Response*, June 2000; page 36)

Although genetically altered seeds can increase yields, reduce the use of chemical pesticides, and prolong freshness, some consumer groups express the concern that the long-term effects of consuming these bio-engineered products have not been studied. Obviously, such products have been tested for toxicity and appear to be safe in that regard. There is no clear evidence that the products *are* harmful. Opponents note that there is no evidence that the products *are not* harmful. Scientists respond that if a product is not proved harmful, it is safe. This does not satisfy the critics of genetically altered food products.

Incidents are beginning to show the unexpected and unintended consequences of genetically altered food. For example, Monarch butterflies died unexpectedly from eating milkweed plants that had been dusted with pollen from genetically engineered Bt corn. (Garden Net at *http://gardennet.com*).

Hygienic Food Preparation and Handling

Cross Contamination

Raw food contains bacteria, including bacteria that can cause food poisoning. If raw food is cooked thoroughly to over 140 degrees fahrenheit (60 degrees centigrade), most of these bacteria will be killed. However, if raw food comes into contact with other food that has already been cooked, or is ready to eat, the bacteria can transfer to this food and cause food poisoning. For this reason, it is important to keep raw food separate from cooked and ready-to-eat food during preparation and storage.

Preparing Food

Separate utensils, chopping boards, and bowls should be used for raw meat and vegetables that are served uncooked. If it is not possible to use separate equipment, that equipment must be washed in hot water and detergent in between use. Wash all fruit and vegetables in clean water before use to remove soil, bacteria, insects, and chemical residues.

Handling Food

Hands should be washed prior to handling food. Raw food that is to be cooked can be safely handled with bare hands, but use utensils such as tongs, spoons, spatulas, or disposable gloves for ready-to-eat food.

Cooking Food

Bacteria multiply rapidly in temperatures ranging between 40 and 140 degrees fahrenheit (5 and 60 degrees centigrade). It is important that foods spend the shortest possible time in this temperature range.

Freezing and Thawing Food

While frozen food is thawing, bacteria in it start multiplying. If the food is refrozen, the bacteria do not die and are still there when the food is thawed again. Rethawed frozen foods tend to have unacceptably high bacteria counts. As a general rule, it is not safe to refreeze thawed food for later use.

(Pamphlet from the United States Department of Public Health)

What Can a Local Church Do?

- Volunteers frequently prepare food for church dinners, and they may not be aware of the need for personal hygiene or the need for hygienic food preparation. Review the practices of volunteer food workers in light of guides from the preceding pamphlet.

- Test the water used in the church kitchen and encourage church members to test water at home. The Environmental Protection Agency (EPA) estimates pesticides contaminate the groundwater in 38 states, polluting the primary source of drinking water.

- Wash fresh fruits and vegetables prior to use to remove chemical residues. The EPA considers 60 percent of all herbicides, 90 percent of all fungicides, and 30 percent of all insecticides are carcinogenic.

- Study your church grounds. How many pesticides, herbicides, and artificial fertilizers are used?

- Observe the rule: When in doubt, throw it out. Never guess that food is safe. Be sure.

Teaching Plans

1. Pray with new incense. Use a baking bread spray to scent your meeting room. Or, program a bread machine to bake fresh bread in time for the beginning of the session. Ask participants to close their eyes and pray the words of Jesus from John 6:27, 33, 47-48, 50-51. Conclude with, "Let us feast on these words of Jesus in our hearts."

2. Reflect. After the prayer ask members to express the feelings evoked by the prayer. Did the bread smell make the words of Jesus more meaningful? What images emerged while you contemplated the Scripture. Did you feel comforted by the fragrance of bread? Did it distract from your devotion?

3. Make a food-guide pyramid that includes: (a) 6 to 11 servings of bread cereal, rice, or pasta; (b) 3 to 5 servings of vegetables; (c) 2 to 4 servings of fruit; (d) 2 to 3 servings of milk, yogurt, or cheese; (e) 2 to 3 servings from the meat, poultry, fish, dry beans, eggs, and nuts group; and (f) a spare consumption of fats, oils, and sweets. Ask participants to write about their own eating habits in general. How do they compare with the federal dietary guidelines?

4. Share favorite stories about food and events associated with food. First share positive happy stories. Then, share some horror stories about food.

5. Discuss. Ask a volunteer to read "Food and the Bible" (page 82). Ask: What role does food play in these Scriptures? How does the perception and use of food reflect the relationships of people with one another and with God?

Ask members to consider what role food played in the life of Jesus. Read Luke 14:16-24 (also in Matthew 22:2-14). What role does food play in this story?

Local Action Report

Johnson Hill United Methodist Church in Eutaw, Alabama, offers a food safety and education program in cooperation with the Tuskegee Extension Office in Greene County. The program connects students interested in growing and preserving food with mentors who have gardening expertise. Students and mentors work together from planting to harvest. Additionally, this project provides food to poor area residents.

Mary Vetrovec serves as a caterer for two United Methodist churches in the Richmond, Virginia, area. She is a paid staff member of Reveille United Methodist Church, a suburban church, and a volunteer for Centenary United Methodist Church, an inner-city congregation.

Vetrovec advises all churches to develop a plan to dispose of food left in the refrigerator. "Youth groups leave leftovers, church staff forget lunches, and any number of other people leave assorted items for various reasons. The result is a very messy refrigerator," says Vetrovec. She suggests putting labels and markers by the appliance with a note that unmarked food will be thrown out in three days.

Noting that Centenary Church receives a lot of food donated from restaurants and food banks, Vetrovec says she is sometimes concerned about how the food has been preserved prior to its arrival at the church. "I always discard food if there's any question," she says. "Refrigerating spoiled food is not going to improve its quality."

The veteran caterer said she has thrown out all wooden cutting boards and always uses a 10 percent bleach solution for cleaning up the kitchen area.